THE I
OF

GW00372862

Natalie

If ever you feel a bit down, heres the book which i use to cheer me up and give me a lift.

You probably wont get half the things written in it (I dont either) but it does make things seem much more positive

Happy 18th

Love
Joe x

Even when the darkest clouds are in the sky
You mustn't sigh and you mustn't cry
Spread a little happiness as you go by
Please try

What's the use of worrying and feeling blue
When days are long keep on smiling through
Spread a little happiness till dreams come true

Surely you'll be wise to make the best of every
blues day
Don't you realize you'll find next Monday or
next Tuesday
Your golden shoes day

Even when the darkest clouds are in the sky
You mustn't sigh and you mustn't cry
Spread a little happiness as you go by

George Gershwin, 1898–1937

THE LITTLE BOOK OF
OPTIMISM

MADELINE SWAN

Published in the United Kingdom in 2009
by Little Books Limited, London W11 3QP

10 9 8 7 6 5 4 3 2 1

Copyright 2009 by Madeline Swann

A CIP catalogue record for this book is available from
the British Library.

ISBN 978 1 906264 0 86

Printed in the UK by CPI Bookmarque Limited, Croydon, Surrey.

Optimists are known to live longer, healthier, happier and richer lives than those who live their lives fearing the worst. For Barack Obama it is change. For Judi Dench it is not taking yourself seriously. For Keith Richard it is the sun, the moon and the Rolling Stones. This book is designed to lift your mood, inspire and entertain you and leave you with a spring in your step. Within these pages you'll find a hundred different definitions of the state of optimism, some sublime, some tongue in cheek, some downright naughty and all designed to cheer. Now more than ever, we all need a bit of optimism. Happy reading.

Comedy is acting out optimism.

Robin Williams, 1951–

Whatever qualities the rich may have,
they can be acquired by anyone with
the tenacity to become rich. The key,
I think, is confidence. Confidence and
an unshakable belief it can be done
and that you are the one to do it.

Felix Dennis, 1947–

Perpetual optimism is
a force multiplier.

Colin Powell, 1937–

It ain't as bad as you think.
It will look better in the morning.

Colin Powell, 1937–

The basis of optimism
is sheer terror.

Oscar Wilde, 1854–1900

The only time I would like to see was the 20s and 30s in America because I love the music and the style and the optimism, I wanted to see New York being built. I wanted to see all that, you know.

Billy Connolly, 1942–

These are the soul's changes. I don't
believe in ageing. I believe in forever
altering one's aspect to the sun.
Hence my optimism.

Virginia Woolf, 1882–1941

I try to avoid looking forward
or backward, and try to keep
looking upward.

Charlotte Bronte, 1816–1855

Nurture your mind with great
thoughts; to believe in the heroic
makes heroes.

Benjamin Disraeli, 1804–1881

Don't judge each day by the harvest
you reap, but by the seeds you plant.

Robert Louis Stevenson, 1850–1894

If you're brilliant and open-minded,
you can start at the top.

Uri Geller, 1946–

Anything's possible if you've got enough nerve.

J. K. Rowling, 1965–

One of the things I learned the hard way was that it doesn't pay to get discouraged. Keeping busy and making optimism a way of life can restore your faith in yourself.

Lucille Ball, 1911–1989

You've got to take the initiative and play your game. In a decisive set, confidence is the difference.

Chris Evert, 1954–

Doctors and scientists said that breaking the four-minute mile was impossible, that one would die in the attempt. Thus, when I got up from the track after collapsing at the finish line, I figured I was dead.

Roger Bannister, 1929–

You must play boldly to win.

Arnold Palmer, 1929–

I've missed more than 9,000 shots in my career. I've lost almost 300 games. 26 times I've been trusted to take the game winning shot and missed. I've failed over and over and over again in my life and that is why I succeed.

Michael Jordan, 1963–

You are never too old to set another
goal or dream a new dream

C. S. Lewis, 1898–1963

Choose a job you love and you will
never have to work a day in your life

Confucius, 551 BC–479 BC

The journey of a thousand miles
begins with but a single step.

Confucius, 551 BC–479 BC

The optimist sees the rose and not its thorns; the pessimist stares at the thorns, oblivious of the rose

Kahlil Gibran 1883–1931

Success consists of going from failure
to failure without loss of enthusiasm.

Winston Churchill, 1874–1965

You see things; and you say "why?" But
I dream of things that never were, and
I say "Why not?"

George Bernard Shaw, 1856–1950

Believe you can
and you're half way there.

Theodore Roosevelt, 1858–1919

What doesn't kill me
only makes me stronger

Friedrich Nietsche, 1844–1900

When one door of happiness closes,
another opens, but often we look
so long at the closed door that we
do not see the one that has been
opened for us.

Helen Keller, 1880–1968

Optimism is the faith that leads to achievement. Nothing can be done without hope and confidence

Helen Keller, 1880–1968

In the middle of every difficulty lies opportunity.

Albert Einstein, 1879–1955

Learn from yesterday, live for today,
hope for tomorrow.

Albert Einstein, 1879–1955

In spite of everything I still believe
that people are really good at heart.
I simply can't build up my hopes on a
foundation consisting of confusion,
misery and death

Anne Frank, 1929–1945

The thing always happens that you really believe in; and the belief in a thing makes it happen.

Frank Lloyd Wright, 1867–1959

As an artist, you dream about accumulating enough successful music to someday do just one greatest-hits album, but to reach the point where you're releasing your second collection of hits is beyond belief.

Gloria Estefan, 1957–

I dreamed impossible dreams. And the dreams turned out beyond anything I could possibly imagine. You know, from my point of view, I'm the luckiest cat on the planet.

Hugh Hefner, 1926–

Business opportunities are like buses,
there's always another one coming.

Richard Branson, 1950—

Think about it! We organise our
minds to obsess about things that don't
amount to a hill of beans.
You be free now!

Bill Clinton, 1946—

I have become my own version of an optimist. If I can't make it through one door, I'll go through another door – or I'll make a door. Something terrific will come no matter how dark the present.

Joan Rivers, 1933–

If they can make penicillin out of
mouldy bread, they can sure make
something out of you.

Muhammad Ali, 1942–

The fragrance always remains on the
hand that gives the rose.

Gandhi, 1869–1948

The most noteworthy thing about gardeners is that they are always optimistic, always enterprising, and never satisfied. They always look forward to doing something better than they have ever done before.

Vita Sackville-West, 1892–1962

Yesterday I dared to struggle.
Today I dare to win.

Bernadette Devlin, 1947–

My mother said to me, "If you become a soldier, you'll be a general; if you become a monk, you'll end up as the Pope." Instead, I became a painter and wound up as Picasso.

Pablo Picasso, 1881–1973

To live happily is an inward power
of the soul.

Aristotle, 384 BC–322 BC

Life is not meant to be easy, my child;
but take courage – it can be delightful.

George Bernard Shaw, 1856–1950

I do not believe in failure. It is not failure if you enjoyed the process.

Oprah Winfrey, 1954–

Cheerfulness is as natural to the heart
of a man in strong health, as color to
his cheek; and wherever there is
habitual gloom, there must be either
bad air, unwholesome food, improperly
severe labor, or erring habits of life"

John Ruskin, 1819–1900

The world is so full of a number of things, I'm sure we should all be as happy as kings.

Robert Louis Stevenson, 1850–1894

Nobody can make you feel inferior
without your consent.

Eleanor Roosevelt, 1884–1962

I am not afraid of storms for I am learning how to sail my ship.

Louisa May Alcott, 1832–1888

Pay no attention to what the critics say.
A statue has never been erected in
honor of a critic.

Jean Sibelius, 1865–1957

I thank you in advance for the great
round of applause I'm about to get.
[Not very confident, then!]

Bo Diddley, 1928–2008

Be daring, be different, be impractical,
be anything that will assert integrity
of purpose and imaginative vision
against the play-it-safers, the
creatures of the commonplace,
the slaves of the ordinary.

Cecil Beaton, 1904–1980

Start by doing what is necessary, then do what is possible, and suddenly you are doing the impossible.

St. Francis of Assisi, 1182–1226

To show your true ability is always, in a sense, to surpass the limits of your ability, to go a little beyond them: to dare, to seek, to invent; it is at such a moment that new talents are revealed, discovered, and realized.

Simone de Beauvoir, 1908–1986

Whatever you can do or dream you
can, begin it.
Boldness has genius, magic and power
in it. Begin it now.

Johann Wolfgang von Goethe, 1749–1832

Beauty, to me, is about being
comfortable in your own skin.
That . . . or a kick-ass red lipstick!

Gwyneth Paltrow, 1972–

What a beautiful day for putting on a kilt, standing upside down in the middle of the road, and saying "How's that for a table lamp?"

Ken Dodd, 1991—

I've got to admit it's getting better.
It's a little better all the time.

Paul Macartney, 1942–

Love is all you need.

Paul McCartney, 1942–

You are all geniuses, and you are all beautiful. You don't need anyone to tell you who you are. You are what you are. Get out there and get peace, think peace, live peace, and breathe peace, and you'll get it as soon as you like.

John Lennon, 9 October 1940–1980

There's nothing you can do that can't
be done.

The Beatles, ALL YOU NEED IS LOVE
Lennon/McCartney

The sun is up, the sky is blue, it's beautiful, and so are you.

The Beatles, DEAR PRUDENCE
Lennon/McCartney

Fashions fade, style is eternal.

Yves Saint Laurent, 1936–2008

Applause, applause, life is our cause.

Joni Mitchell, ALL I WANT 1943—

Zest is the secret of all beauty.
There is no beauty that is attractive
without zest.

Christian Dior, 1905–1957

Don't fall for a magic wand, we humans got it all, we perform the miracles.

Kate Bush, THEM HEAVY PEOPLE 1958–

When the spirit moves me, I can do many wondrous things.

Van Morrison, DID YE GET HEALED
1945–

My friends, as I have discovered
myself, there are no disasters, only
opportunities. And, indeed,
opportunities for fresh disasters.

Boris Johnson, 1964–

Tremendous, little short of superb.
On cracking form.
[after being sacked of his role in the
Tory shadow cabinet]

Boris Johnson, 1964–

I can only go one way.
I've not got a reverse gear.
[Labour Party Conference speech,
30 September 2003]

Tony Blair, 1953–

Some people create with words, or with music, or with a brush and paints. I like to make something beautiful when I run. I like to make people stop and say, "I've never seen anyone run like that before." It's more then just a race, it's a style. It's doing something better then anyone else. It's being creative.

Steve Prefontaine, 1951–1975

To give anything less than your best is
to sacrifice the gift

Steve Prefontaine, 1951–1975

Life's battles don't always go to the
strongest or fastest man,
But sooner or later the man who wins
is the fellow who thinks he can.

Anonymous

Success isn't how far you got,
but the distance you travelled from
where you started.

Proverb

Many of life's failures are people who
did not realize how close they were to
success when they gave up.

Thomas Edison, 1847–1931

I have this one little saying, when things get too heavy just call me helium, the lightest known gas to man.

Jimi Hendrix, 1942–1970

It is necessary to relax your muscles when you can. Relaxing your brain is fatal

Sir Stirling Moss, 1929–

The great thing about rock and roll is
that someone like me can be a star.

Elton John, 1947–

The whole point of being in this business and being blessed and being successful is that you're able to do things for your friends or your family, which means that they can have something special in their lives, too.

Elton John 1947–

You've got the sun, you've got the moon, and you've got the Rolling Stones.

Keith Richards, 1943–

Change will not come if we wait for
some other person or some other time.
We are the ones we've been waiting for.
We are the change that we seek.

Barack Obama, 1961–

Focusing your life solely on making
a buck shows a certain poverty of
ambition. It asks too little of yourself.
Because it's only when you hitch
your wagon to something larger
than yourself that you realize
your true potential.

Barack Obama, 1961–

All free men, wherever they may live,
are citizens of Berlin. And therefore, as
a free man, I take pride in the words
"Ich bin ein Berliner!"

John F. Kennedy, 1917–1963

And so, my fellow Americans, ask not what your country can do for you; ask what you can do for your country.

John F. Kennedy, 1917–1963

Peace is a daily, a weekly, a monthly process, gradually changing opinions, slowly eroding old barriers, quietly building new structures.

John F. Kennedy, 1917–1963

"Why", ask instead, "Why not".

John F. Kennedy, 1917–1963

The time to repair a roof is when the sun is shining.

John F. Kennedy, 1917–1963

I feel very adventurous. There are so many doors to be opened, and I'm not afraid to look behind them.

Elizabeth Taylor, 1932–

I think you should take your job seriously, but not yourself — that is the best combination.

Judi Dench, 1934–

Everyone has the right to walk from
one end of the city to the other in
secure and beautiful spaces. Everybody
has the right to go by public transport.
Everybody has the right to an
unhampered view down their street,
not full of railings, signs and rubbish.

Richard Rogers, 1933–

Be daring, be different, be impractical,
be anything that will assert integrity
of purpose and imaginative vision
against the play-it-safers, the creatures
of the commonplace, the slaves
of the ordinary.

Cecil Beaton, 1904–1980

I'd like to think that the actions we take today will allow others in the future to discover the wonders of landscapes we helped protect but never had the chance to enjoy ourselves.

Annie Leibovitz, 1949–

Consult not your fears but your hopes and your dreams. Think not about your frustrations, but about your unfulfilled potential. Concern yourself not with what you tried and failed in, but with what it is still possible for you to do.

Pope John XXIII 1881–1963

If we want a love message to be heard, it has got to be sent out. To keep a lamp burning, we have to keep putting oil in it.

Mother Teresa, 1910–1997

I've realized that being happy is a choice. You never want to rub anybody the wrong way or not be fun to be around, but you have to be happy. When I get logical and I don't trust my instincts – Thats when I get in trouble.

Angelina Jolie, 1975–

"Beauty is truth, truth beauty,"
– that is all ye know on earth,
and all ye need to know.

John Keats, 1795–1821

You will never be happier than you expect. To change your happiness, change your expectation.

Bette Davis, 1908–1989

Money can't buy you happiness, but it does bring you a more pleasant form of misery.

Spike Milligan 1918–2002

Thousands of candles can be lighted
from a single candle. And the life of
the candle will not be shortened.
Happiness never decreases
by being shared.

Buddha, 563 BCE to 483 BCE

Whoever is happy will make others
happy, too.

Mark Twain, 1835–21, 1910

Always Look on the Bright
Side of Life

Eric Idle, 1943–

Optimism is the cheerful frame of
mind that enables a kettle to sing,
though in hot water up to its nose.

Anon

Emancipate yourself from mental
slavery, none but ourselves can
free our minds.

Bob Marley, REDEMPTION SONG
1945–1981

Freedom of choice is a universal
principle to which there should
be no exceptions.

Mikhail Gorbachev 1931–

Laughter is the shortest distance
between two people.

Victor Borge, 1909–2000

Sunshine is delicious, rain is refreshing,
wind braces up, snow is exhilarating;
there is no such thing as bad weather,
only different kinds of good weather.

John Ruskin, 1819 –1900

I am prepared to go anywhere,
provided it be forward.

David Livingstone, 1813–1873

One small step for man
one giant leap for mankind.

Neil Armstrong, 1930–

A pessimist is one who makes
difficulties of his opportunities and an
optimist is one who makes
opportunities of his difficulties

Harry Truman, 1884–1972

From birth, man carries the weight of gravity on his shoulders. He is bolted to earth. But man has only to sink beneath the surface and he is free.

Jacques Yves Cousteau, 1910–1997

There is not spot of ground,
however arid, bare, or ugly,
that cannot be tamed.

Gertrude Jekyll, 1843–1932

He who fears being conquered
is sure of defeat.

Napoleon Bonaparte, 1769 – 1821

When two people love each other, they don't look at each other, they look in the same direction.

Ginger Rogers, 1911–1995

The thing always happens that you really believe in; and the belief in a thing makes it happen.

Frank Lloyd Wright, 1867–1959

Imagination is the highest kite
one can fly.

Lauren Bacall, 1924–

We are all in the gutter, but some of us are looking at the stars

Oscar Wilde, 1854–1900

What are days for?
Days are where we live.
They come, they wake us
Time and time over.
They are to be happy in:
Where can we live but days?

Philip Larkin, 1922–1985

It's never too late to become what
you might have been.

George Clooney, 1961–

Lead me not into temptation;
I can find the way myself.

Rita Mae Brown, 1944–

Imperfection is beauty, madness is genius, and it is better to absolutely ridiculous than absolutely boring.

Marilyn Monroe, 1926–1962

May the road rise to meet you.
May the wind be always at your back.
May the sun shine warm upon your face,
And rains fall soft upon your fields.
And until we meet again
May God hold you in the hollow
of His hand.